MAY 1 5 2006

W9-AAE-094

★ IT'S MY STATE! ★
Nevada

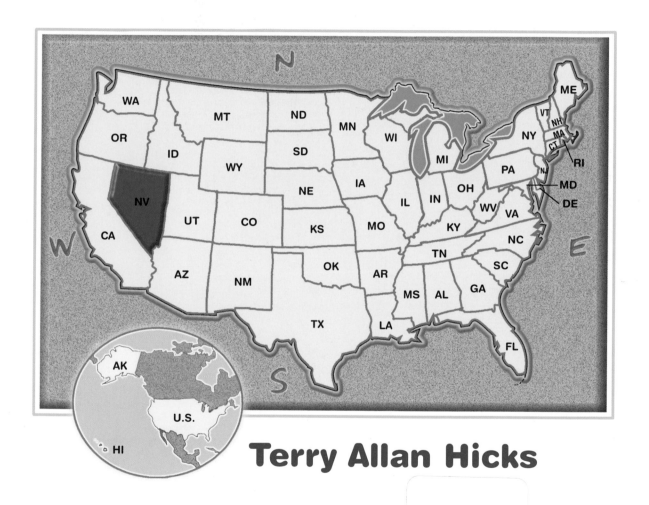

Terry Allan Hicks

 Marshall Cavendish
Benchmark
New York

Series Consultant

David G. Vanderstel, Ph.D., Executive Director National Council on Public History

With thanks to Barbara Slivac, Curator of Education, Nevada State Museum & History Society, for her expert review of the manuscript.

Marshall Cavendish Benchmark
99 White Plains Road
Tarrytown, New York 10591-9001
www.marshallcavendish.us

Library of Congress Cataloging-in-Publication Data

Hicks, Terry Allan.
Nevada / by Terry Allan Hicks.
p. cm. -- (It's my state!)
Summary: "Surveys the history, geography, and economy of Nevada, as well as the diverse ways of life of its people"--Provided by publisher.
Includes index.
ISBN 0-7614-1860-1
1. Nevada--Juvenile literature. I. Title. II. Series.

F841.3.H53 2005
979.3--dc22

2004030035

Photo research by Candlepants, Inc.

Cover photograph: Creatas

Back cover: The license plate shows Nevada's postal abbreviation, followed by its year of statehood.

The photographs in this book are used by permission and through the courtesy of: Photo Researchers, Inc. : Kenneth W. Fink, 4 (top); Tom and Pat Leeson, 4 (middle); Richard W. Brooks, 4 (bottom); Craig K. Lorenz, 5 (top); Dan Suzio, 5 (middle); Chris Butler, 5 (bottom); Tom McHugh, 21 (bottom); Charles D. Winter, 70 (top). Index Stock Imagery : Mick Roessler, 8; Charlie Borland, 19. Corbis : 32, 34, 41 (top), 41 (bottom); D. Boone, 10; Gerald French, 11; Phil Schermeister, 12; David Muench, 13, 20 (middle), 20 (bottom); Lester Lefkowitz, 15, 71 (bottom); Rick Doyle, 16; Nigel Francis, 17; Kennan Ward, 20 (top); Royalty Free, 21 (top); Scott T. Smith, 24; Bettmann, 26, 37, 39, 51 (bottom); Tom Bean, 40; Morton Beebe, 45, 55, 64, 67; Reuters, 50 (middle), 50 (bottom); ZUMA / Mike Valdez, 62; Galen Rowell, 66; SABA / David Butow, 68, 72, 70 (middle); Jim Sugar, 69; Richard T. Nowitz, 71 (top); Patrick Bennett, 71 (middle). The Image Works : A. Vossberg, 14; James Marshall, 44. Minden Pictures : Tim Fitzharris, 22; Jim Brandenburg, 21 (middle). Animals Animals : Lynn Stone, 23. Getty Images / Editorial: The Image Bank, 36; Time Life Pictures, 51 (middle). Nevada Commission on Tourism : 42, 47, 52, 54, 56, 59, 70, 74. Buddy Mays : 53. Nevada Historical Society : 50 (top), 51 (top).

Book design by Anahid Hamparian

Printed in Italy

1 3 5 6 4 2

Contents

A Quick Look at Nevada

Nickname: The Silver State
Population: 2,241,154 (2003 estimate)
Statehood: October 31, 1864

Tree: Single-Leaf Piñon

This tough, hardy pine thrives even in the coarse, rocky soil of the high mountains. The pine nuts that come from the tree were once an important food source for the Native Americans of the region, and pine nuts are still used in many recipes today.

Bird: Mountain Bluebird

Mountain bluebirds are found all over the western part of North America, usually at altitudes of 5, 000 feet. They eat insects, such as grasshoppers and crickets, and often hover in the air while feeding.

Flower: Sagebrush

This tough, hardy bush, with its pale yellow flowers and its sweet smell, can grow in places too harsh for other plants. When winter comes, sagebrush may be the only food Nevada's cattle and sheep can find on the open range. The Native Americans of Nevada have used sagebrush to make everything from medicine to candles.

Animal: Bighorn Sheep

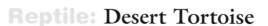

The bighorn—also known as the Nelson sheep—is well adapted to life in Nevada, because it can go a long time without water. An adult male may stand around 4 feet tall and weigh 175 pounds. The males have long, heavy, curving horns that they use to fight other males during mating season. The females have shorter spiky horns.

Reptile: Desert Tortoise

The desert tortoise is the largest reptile in the southwestern United States. This reptile can live to be more than seventy years old. It survives in the harsh conditions of southern Nevada—hot in the summer, cold in the winter—by spending much of its life in underground burrows. Nevada's desert tortoise population has fallen sharply in recent years, partly because of illegal hunting and partly because tortoises are killed by cars.

Fossil: Ichthyosaur (*Shonisaurus populalis*)

Hundreds of millions of years ago, these now-extinct reptiles swam in warm, shallow salt seas that covered what is now the Nevada desert. Many ichthyosaur fossils—hardened remains—have been found in Berlin, in the central part of the state. The ichthyosaur was officially named the state fossil in 1977.

NEVADA

Owyhee

Owyhee Desert

BILK CREEK MOUNTAINS

Black Rock Desert

QUINN RIVER

THE LAVA BEDS

Winnemucca

HUMBOLDT RIVER

Battle Mountain

INDEPENDENCE MOUNTAINS

Elko

Spring Creek

West Wendover

HUNTINGTON RIVER

RUBY MOUNTAINS

Pyramid Lake

Humboldt Salt Marsh

Sparks

Reno

Carson City

Lake Tahoe

Walker Lake

Hawthorne

Eureka

Ely

TOIYABE RANGE

Ruth Copper Pit

MONITOR RANGE

HUMBOLDT-TOIYABE NATIONAL FOREST

Lunar Crater

EXCELSIOR MOUNTAINS

Boundary Peak

Tonopah

Caliente

DESERT NATIONAL WILDLIFE RANGE

DELMAR MOUNTAINS

DEATH VALLEY NATIONAL PARK

Nevada Military Test Site

Beatty

Mesquite

VIVA!

Amargosa Desert

Las Vegas

Lake Mead

HOOVER DAM

Boulder City

Laughlin

COLORADO RIVER

N

W

E

S

1 The Silver State

Nevada is a huge state—the seventh-largest in the country—with an area of 110,540 square miles. It is also one of the most beautiful states, with snowcapped mountains, clear blue lakes, and large stretches of desert where wild horses roam. For centuries, this amazing place was nearly empty, because its harsh climate made settling here difficult. But in recent years, millions of people have discovered Nevada, making it one of the nation's great tourist attractions, and its fastest-growing state.

Nevada's Borders
North: Oregon and Idaho
South: Arizona
East: Utah
West: California

The Sierra Nevada

Nevada takes its name from the Sierra Nevada, the great mountain range that cuts across the northwestern section of the state. (The word *nevada* is a Spanish word that means "snowy" or "snow-covered.") The Sierra Nevada began to form about 150 million years ago, when huge masses of rock began to shift and push upward and volcanoes spewed molten lava that cooled to

The peaks of the Sierra Nevada. Their name means "snow-covered mountains" in Spanish.

form granite mountains. The tall peaks of the Sierra Nevada form a natural barrier between Nevada and its western neighbor California. The highest point in Nevada, the 13,140-foot Boundary Peak, lies exactly on the border between the two states.

Nevada has never been an easy place to live. The difficulty of traveling through the Sierra Nevada kept settlers

Nevada's landscape was shaped by water and wind. The retreating glaciers of the Ice Age carved deep lakes and canyons in the Sierra Nevada. And millions of years of wind and water wore down rocks to create the fine sand that now covers much of the state.

away for many years. Even today, with modern highways and four-wheel-drive vehicles, heavy snows sometimes shut off entire towns for days or even weeks at a time. And yet Native Americans have made the Sierra Nevada their home for thousands of years. This is also where settlement by white people in Nevada began.

This little corner of northwestern Nevada, in the shadow of the Sierra Nevada, is still a very important place. This is where you will find Reno, which is also known as the "biggest little city in the world." Reno has only about 190,000 residents, but about half a million visitors travel to the city each month. Most of them come to enjoy a pastime that has been the backbone of the state's economy for more than half a century: gambling.

But this part of Nevada has much more to offer than roulette wheels and card tables. Tourists also come to remember the days of Nevada's rich past, in places like Virginia City, which works hard to preserve the heritage of the mining days that gave Nevada the nickname "the Silver State." Over a hundred years ago, when Virginia City was a very profitable silver mining town, its population was around

More than 10,000 years ago, during the Ice Age, the now-extinct Lake Lahontan covered 8,450 square miles of western Nevada. This huge prehistoric lake was formed by Ice Age glaciers, and it mostly disappeared when the glaciers withdrew. Today, Pyramid Lake, Walker Lake, and a few smaller bodies of water are all that remain of Lahontan.

Virginia City is now a very small town, but it was once the center of Nevada's silver rush.

30,000. However, fewer than a thousand people live there today.

Just fifteen miles south of Virginia City is another former mining center: Carson City. This is a tourist attraction, too, with museums and restored buildings from pioneer days. But this is also Nevada's capital, where lawmakers meet to decide on the most important issues facing the state.

West of Carson City, along the California-Nevada state line, is Lake Tahoe. The 193-square-mile lake is famous for its sparkling blue water. It is said that the water is so clear you can sometimes see objects 75 feet below the surface. The shores of Lake Tahoe are lined with resorts that draw

Lake Tahoe is high in the mountains—6,229 feet above sea level—but it never freezes over, even in the coldest winter. That is because it is one of the deepest lakes in the world. At its deepest point, the bottom of the lake is about 1,645 feet deep.

Lake Tahoe holds enough water to cover the entire state of California.

boaters, swimmers, and hikers in the summer. In the winter, skiers and snowboarders come to the area to enjoy the deep powder snow. The 1960 Winter Olympics were held there, at Squaw Valley.

The Great Basin

Most of Nevada is taken up by a 200,000-square-mile region known as the Great Basin. The Great Basin stretches from the foothills of the Sierra Nevada all the way to the Rocky Mountains on the state's eastern border. This low-lying area was formed millions of years ago, when movements in the earth raised the surrounding areas higher. The Great Basin is shaped like a huge bowl, which is how it got its name. Like a bowl, the basin traps water. Rivers in most parts of the world flow outward, toward oceans and lakes. But in this region, most of the streams and rivers flow inward. Many end in low, marshy areas called sinks, or in stretches of dry, cracked clay called playas.

The northern section of Nevada is "cowboy country," where many ranchers still drive their herds the old-fashioned way, on

The wagon trains of the Old West often followed the Humboldt River in northern Nevada.

horseback. Sometimes ranchers and their herds stop traffic on the highways on the way to and from the ranches. The area around Elko, in the northeastern corner of the state, also has huge open-pit mining operations that have some of the largest gold deposits in the world.

Stretching south from cowboy country is a huge expanse of flatlands. Much of this area is semidesert—dry land where only the toughest plants and animals can survive. Cutting across this area are more than a hundred small, steep-sided mountain ranges that run from north to south. Very few people live here, and some counties are almost uninhabited. A stretch of

A local rancher discovered Lehman Caves, with their beautiful limestone formations, in 1885.

The "loneliest road in America"—Nevada's Highway 50

Highway 50, outside Fallon, is sometimes called "the loneliest road in America," because you can drive parts of it for hours without seeing another human being.

But this does not mean there is nothing going on out there in the Nevada countryside. Huge stretches of the Silver State are owned by the federal government. The government uses them for many different purposes, such as testing new weapons.

Near the tiny town of Rachel, in south-central Nevada, is a military base known as Area 51. This base is surrounded by a lot of mystery. It is believed that the government conducts secret experiments at the base. Some people even think Area 51 holds alien spacecraft that crashed in the nearby desert.

Why are parts of Nevada so empty? The reason is simple: There is just not enough water to support a large population. But in the southern Nevada desert you will find a huge body of water. The water comes from the Colorado River, and is controlled and directed by the huge Hoover Dam, located along the Nevada-Arizona border.

This enormous concrete dam controls the flooding of the Colorado River and supplies precious water for homes and farms. When it was built, in the 1930s, it created a brand-new lake in the Nevada desert: the 115-mile-long Lake Mead.

As many as 10 million people come every year to enjoy the clear blue lake in the middle of the bone-dry desert. Power generators at the Hoover Dam also

Hoover Dam is 726 feet high and 1,244 feet long.

A water skier races across the surface of Lake Mead.

produce large amounts of electricity, and that is a good thing—because rising from the desert only about 25 miles to the northwest are the glittering neon-lit towers of Las Vegas.

Las Vegas, located in southern Nevada, is the largest city in the state. It is home to the world-famous Las Vegas Strip—a 3-mile-long stretch of road lined with hotels and casinos. Las Vegas is known as the Entertainment Capital of the World. Many singers, dancers, circus performers, and other "acts" can be seen on the stages of Las Vegas.

> The Great Basin is a "cold" desert. But the southwestern part of Nevada is part of a very different type of desert. The Mojave Desert—which stretches from Nevada to California's Death Valley and includes Las Vegas—is the hottest, driest desert in the United States.

Many people come to Las Vegas to live and work. It is now the fastest-growing city in the United States. New roads and housing developments are being built everywhere you look. What was once a small, sleepy town now extends far out into what was once empty desert.

A view of brightly-lit Las Vegas at night.

The Silver State

Climate

The Silver State has one of the world's most extreme climates. Nevada is the driest state in the country, with average precipitation—the moisture that falls from the sky in the form of rain, snow, sleet, and hail—of just 7 inches a year. (The national average is 40 inches.) Yet some parts of the Sierra Nevada get more than 80 inches of precipitation in a year. And in many parts of the state, sudden thunderstorms can send flash floods racing down on unsuspecting hikers.

Temperatures in the state can also vary. The temperature in the south can shift wildly in a single day, from 80 degrees Fahrenheit in the afternoon to only a few degrees above freezing at night. The desert town of Laughlin recorded a blistering 125 degrees one June day in 1994. But Nevada also experiences cold temperatures. The coldest temperature recorded was on January 9, 1937. On that day, thermometers in the northern town of San Jacinto fell to a bone-chilling -50 degrees.

Despite these wide variations in temperature and precipitation, Nevada's climate is very consistent in one way: There is almost always a lot of sunlight. The state's southern desert may get as many as 320 sunny days in a year. Nevada has a harsh and extreme environment, but that has not kept people from living here. It has also not prevented an amazing range of plants and animals—some of them found nowhere else—from making Nevada their home.

Wild Nevada

An amazing number of plants and animals survive—and even thrive—in this harsh environment. Even in the parched desert, you will see sagebrush, yucca, Joshua trees, and more than two dozen types of cactus. In places where water is more plentiful, bright, colorful wildflowers, like Indian paintbrush, shooting stars, and yellow and white violets, dot the countryside.

Many parts of the Silver State are almost completely tree-less, but piñon, juniper, pine, and fir trees grow in the mountains. Ancient bristlecone pines, some of them more than four thousand years old, cling to the steep slopes of Wheeler Peak, in Great Basin National Park. All over the state, wherever there is a little water, alder, chokecherry, and cottonwood trees can be found. In the autumn, their leaves turn yellow, bringing a welcome touch of color to the landscape.

Balsamroot flowers add color to the Nevada landscape.

Plants & Animals

American White Pelican

Every spring, thousands of American white pelicans descend on the waterways of western Nevada, especially Pyramid Lake, to breed. These water birds can be 50 inches in length and have a 110-inch wingspan, and they catch fish in their huge beaks while swimming. When the weather turns cold, they head south with their young.

Bristlecone Pine

The bristlecone is a tough pine tree with sharp needles and prickly cones. It grows in the high mountains of Nevada and California. These pines are probably the oldest living things on earth. One bristlecone that was cut down on the slopes of Wheeler Peak in 1964 is believed to have been more than 4,000 years old.

Yucca

Yucca are tall plants that can be found throughout the southern Nevada desert. They have white or purple flowers and tall, spiky leaves that store water for the plant to use during dry periods. The Native Americans ate the flowers and leaves of the yucca. The plant's roots can be made into soap.

Wild Horse

In Nevada's pioneer days, horses sometimes escaped from their owners to live in the wild. These horses—often called mustangs—remained wild, traveled in herds and bred with each other. Today, as many as 45,000 of their wild descendants roam free in the state's wide-open spaces.

Mule Deer

The mule deer takes it name from its big mulelike ears, which move constantly. This desert dweller has a very good sense of smell, which it uses to find water underground. Using its large hooves, it can dig for water at depths of up to 2 feet.

Sidewinder

The poisonous sidewinder, one of seven species of rattlesnake in Nevada, is named for the unusual way it moves. It moves its body sideways in a looping motion, making a distinctive S-shaped mark in the sand.

Among the large animals that make their home in Nevada are bighorn sheep, pronghorn antelope, elk, mule deer, mustangs, and small donkeys called burros. Smaller animals include cottontail rabbits, coyotes, foxes, and porcupines. Nevada also has plenty of reptiles:

The pika, relative of the rabbit, is one of many small animals that survive in Nevada's harsh environment.

lizards, and snakes, like the desert tortoise, the Western fence lizard, rattlesnakes, and the poisonous Gila monster.

Many parts of Nevada are growing so fast that humans sometimes come into conflict with wildlife. Coyotes have been known to drink from suburban swimming pools, and rattlesnakes sometimes sleep under people's cars on hot days. And if you are hiking in Nevada's many wilderness areas, you should keep a careful eye out for bears and mountain lions, as well as the state's many poisonous snakes.

Nevada's lakes and rivers are filled with fish, including many types—such as largemouth bass, perch, and trout—that sport fisherman love to catch and eat. The cui-ui (its name is pronounced kwee-wee) is a rare fish found only in Nevada's Pyramid Lake. The cui-ui has been listed as an endangered species since 1967, but conservation efforts are helping to increase its population.

Many birds—including a number of water birds, like

Wild donkeys, called burros, graze—eat—in the desert.

ducks, geese, and pelicans—fill Nevada's skies. Great birds of prey, such as falcons, bald and golden eagles, and owls can be found in the state. Nevada is also home to smaller birds like bluebirds, hummingbirds, and doves.

Nevada's fast-growing human population threatens the habitats of some of these plants and animals. Some of Nevada's species, for example, the steamboat buckwheat, the Lahontan cutthroat trout, the bald eagle, and the Pahute green gentian, are considered endangered or threatened. Many of these species are in trouble because fast-growing towns and cities are being built in their natural habitats. The state tries to protect them from people who might harm them, either on purpose or by mistake.

Nevadans are also concerned about the need to protect their unique natural environment. For example, they have passed important laws to protect the state's wild horses, to keep Lake Tahoe free from pollution, and to set aside large wilderness areas as nature preserves. The people of Nevada know that their natural environment is one of their greatest assets. As their state grows, they are determined to protect their air, and especially their valuable water, from the effects of pollution.

2 From the Beginning

The First Nevadans

The first people who lived in the area that includes present-day Nevada were early Native Americans, now known as Paleo-Indians. They are believed to have been descendants of people who crossed a land bridge that once connected Asia and North America, tens of thousands of years ago. Over time, they spread out all over the Americas. The Paleo-Indians left behind many traces of their way of life, such as stone weapons and fishing nets. They also left behind rock carvings called petroglyphs. These artifacts show that the Paleo-Indians were living in the area as early as 10,000 B.C.E.

Then, sometime between 300 B.C.E. and 100 C.E., a different group of Native American people, known as the Anasazi, came to the region. (Today many refer to the Anasazi as the Ancestral Pueblo peoples.) Nobody really knows where they came from. By about 700 C.E., the Anasazi were building elaborate dwellings, called pueblos. These buildings were made out of sun-dried clay bricks and could be found in several areas of

Native Americans carved these images, called petroglyphs, into the rocks thousands of years ago.

the Southwest. Some of the Anasazi pueblos had as many as one hundred rooms. The largest Anasazi community may have been home to almost 20,000 people.

The Anasazi were farmers. They built dams on the rivers to irrigate—bring water to—their fields of beans, corn, and squash. They were also skilled artists, creating beautiful black-and-white pottery and intricately woven baskets that are now often seen in museums.

And then, about 1150 C.E., these remarkable people simply disappeared. Were they driven out by famine, or drought, or war with neighboring Native Americans? The question has fascinated archaeologists and historians for many years, but nobody knows the answer.

In the 1920s, archeologists rediscovered an important group of Anasazi ruins in the Nevada desert. Just ten years later, as workers raced to dig up as many artifacts as they could, much of the "Lost City" of the Anasazi was covered forever by the rising waters of the manmade Lake Mead.

Archeologists at work in the "Lost City" of the Anasazi in 1926

By the early sixteenth century, the region that includes present-day Nevada was inhabited by Native Americans unrelated to the Anasazi. The Northern Paiute lived in what is now western Nevada, while the Southern Paiute lived in the southeastern portion. The Shoshone made their homes in the eastern and central sections of present-day Nevada. The Washo lived around the Lake Tahoe region.

Most of these peoples were nomadic hunters and gatherers. They traveled across the mountains and deserts in search of food. They followed herds of animals and hunted antelope and bighorn sheep. They also trapped rabbits and water birds, and ate pine nuts and other plants. The Native Americans' way of life remained unchanged for centuries, until European explorers and settlers began to arrive.

The Coming of the Europeans

The first non-Native American to set foot in the region was probably Father Francisco Garcés, a Spanish priest who passed through on his way to California in 1776. The Spaniards claimed the region that now includes Nevada as theirs, but they never really established settlements there.

Many more white people passed through the future state, never staying long. In 1827, Jedediah Smith, an American "mountain man," led a party of fur trappers from Utah on the difficult journey across Nevada to California and back again. John Charles Frémont, a U.S. army officer and mapmaker, crisscrossed what is now present-day Nevada in 1843 and 1844. He named the Carson River for his guide, the great frontiersman Christopher "Kit" Carson.

In 1848, a treaty with Mexico gave the United States

control of most of the Southwest, including the land that is now Nevada. By then, thousands of American settlers were already headed west in wagon trains, to settle in Oregon and California. Even more came when gold was discovered at Sutter's Mill in northern California. Suddenly, thousands of people began pouring into the California gold fields. Many of them used a route that passed through the region that is now Nevada. The trip was long and dangerous, taking the would-be gold miners across hundreds of miles of burning desert, then through the high passes of the mountains.

In October 1846, tragedy struck the Sierra Nevada. The Donner Party, a group of settlers, was trapped in the mountains by an early snow. Almost half of the eighty-seven people in the party died, and the survivors, half-mad with hunger, were driven to cannibalism—eating the bodies of those who had died—in order to survive.

In 1850, Congress created the Utah Territory—a large area of land that included most of present-day Nevada. Some of the first non-Native Americans who came to the territory to stay were members of the Church of Jesus Christ of Latter-Day Saints, a religious group also known as the Mormons. Mormons began settling there in the hope of practicing their religion in peace. One group of Mormons founded a trading post called Mormon Station (or Reese's Station) in the Carson Valley in 1851. It was the first permanent settlement by white people in the land that would become Nevada.

In 1859, two prospectors found an enormous vein of gold

running beneath the Sierra Nevada. Another prospector, Henry Paige Comstock—known to the locals as "Old Pancake"—swore the land where they had found the gold was his. Many people doubted his claim, but to this day, the find is called the Comstock Lode.

The discovery set off another gold rush, but the prospectors working the Comstock soon made an even more incredible discovery. The gold they were digging up was mixed with a blue-black "mud." They complained about the mud, until someone realized it contained silver. The silver was worth far more than Old Pancake's gold. It was, in fact, the richest silver deposit ever found in the United States.

When the news of the silver strike reached the outside world, even more fortune-seekers began flooding into the region. Scratching for silver in the rocky ground was hard, dirty, dangerous work, and many men died from mining accidents, disease, or harsh weather. Some say the winter of 1859 through 1860 was the worst. Heavy snow closed the Sierra Nevada passes and food supplies could not get through. The silver fields were also dangerous because they were a lawless place. Disputes were settled with fists, with knives, or with guns.

Despite these hardships, entire towns grew up practically overnight. Virginia City, which had been little more than a few prospectors' tents in 1859, had a population of 15,000 by 1863. There were hotels, theaters, churches, gambling halls, and saloons. The city even had its own newspaper, the *Territorial Enterprise*. A young reporter for the *Enterprise*, Samuel Clemens, later became world-famous as Mark Twain, the author of *The Adventures of Tom Sawyer* and *The Adventures of Huckleberry Finn*.

Make a Pioneer Sun Bonnet

Pioneers heading out west on the wagon trains made simple hats and bonnets to protect themselves from the sun and to keep some of the dust out of their hair. By following these instructions you can make your own simple bonnet.

What You Need

A piece of cotton or linen fabric—about 20 inches square
A ruler
A pen
Scissors
4 feet of ribbon (no wider than 1/2 an inch)
1 foot of string, thread, or twine

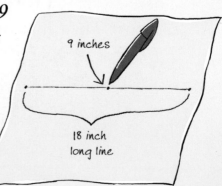

Spread the fabric flat on your work surface, with the outer side (the side with the designs or color) face down. (Be sure to use newspapers or old magazines underneath your fabric to protect your work surface.) Use the ruler to draw an 18-inch line in the center of the fabric. Make a mark on the line at 9 inches—that should be the center of your line.

Tie the string to the pen. Make sure that the distance from the end of the string to the pen is only 9 inches. Hold the end of the string without the pen at the center (9-inch) mark on your line. Stretch out the string so that it is straight and use the pen to draw a

9 inches

18 inch long line

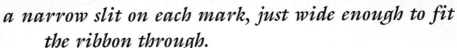

circle on your fabric. The edges of your circle should touch the ends of the 18-inch line.

Cut out your circle with the scissors.

Using the ruler and pen, make marks around the circle, about 1-1/2 inches from the edge. Make the marks about 1 inch long and leave a space of about 1 inch between each mark. Cut a narrow slit on each mark, just wide enough to fit the ribbon through.

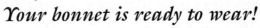

Turn the fabric over so that the outer side is facing you. Weave the ribbon through the slits, alternating over and under, over and under. You should leave a few inches at both ends of the ribbon.

Place the bonnet on your head, a little toward the back. Pull the ribbons gently and use your hands to tighten the bonnet to a comfortable fit. (You can have an adult or a friend help you do this.) Tie the ends of the ribbon into a little bow.

Your bonnet is ready to wear!

Miners faced great danger as they searched for silver deep underground.

The silver rush and the increase in white settlement brought trouble for the Native Americans. These two groups—the settlers and the Native Americans—did not understand each others' ways. This sometimes led to violence. The prospectors often stole the Natives' land, hunted their game, and cut down the trees that they used for tools, homes, and food.

In 1860, a group of Paiute—angered by the kidnaping of two young girls from their village—killed three white men. The white settlers put together a group to fight the Paiute. But the settlers were ambushed by the Paiute near Pyramid Lake. Seventy-six settlers were killed, in the first engagement of what came to be called the Pyramid Lake War. The settlers recovered and, aided by U.S. Army troops, killed about 160 Paiute. The war lasted only a few months, and it ended Native American resistance in Nevada forever. The federal government forced the Native Americans of Nevada to move to reservations that had been set aside for them. One Nevada group, the Northern Paiute, refused to live on a reservation, and settled on wilderness lands in southern Utah instead.

On March 2, 1861, in an attempt to stop the lawlessness in

the area, the government created the Nevada Territory, separate from Utah. Carson City served as the territorial capital. But within weeks, a conflict on the other side of the country—the Civil War—was to change Nevada's destiny.

The Civil War began in 1861 and lasted until 1865. The Northern states—known as the Union—fought against the Southern states, which were called the Confederacy. Many battles were fought and hundreds of thousands of lives were lost during the Civil War. The battles were fought thousands of miles away, but Nevada played an important role in the war. The Union used Comstock silver to help pay for soldiers and supplies.

On October 31, 1864, President Abraham Lincoln declared Nevada the thirty-sixth state. Nevada's new representatives raced to the nation's capital, Washington, D.C., just in time to vote for the Thirteenth Amendment to the United States Constitution. This amendment ended slavery in America once and for all. The Southern states rejoined the United States and the country began to heal.

Nevada is sometimes called the "Battle Born State," because it was the only state created during the Civil War.

As the Civil War came to an end, Nevada continued to grow at a fast pace. The mines of Nevada were now producing silver worth an estimated $23 million every year. In 1869, the Transcontinental Railroad was completed. The railroad connected Omaha, Nebraska, and the cities of the East, with the fast-growing town of Sacramento, California. A cross-country trip that had once taken six difficult months could now be made in under a week. Besides bringing new people to Nevada, the railroad also helped to create towns.

Many towns and cities were built along the railroad line in different parts of Nevada. These included places such as Reno and Elko.

People kept coming to the state. Many were Americans from midwestern or eastern states. But by the mid-1870s, nearly half of all Nevadans had been born outside the United States. Among them were Irish miners, German farmers, French-Canadian lumberjacks, Chinese railway workers, and Basque sheepherders.

In the early-morning hours of October 5, 1870, five masked men stopped a train outside Reno and rode off with a strongbox containing $50,000 worth of gold and silver. This is believed to be the first train robbery in the American West.

Nevada was very important to the economy of the United States. The country's currency or money was based largely on

When silver was discovered in the Sierra Nevada, entire towns appeared, practically overnight.

the silver dollar. These dollars were minted from Nevada silver. But then the federal government, in Washington, D.C., changed the way it issued money. Now the U.S. dollar would be based on gold, not silver.

Boom and Bust

Nevada's history is like a roller-coaster ride—"boom" times of wealth and prosperity, followed by "busts" that bring hard times. The Comstock boom was followed by the bust of the 1880s, when the U.S. government switched the country's currency from silver to gold. Also, the silver in the Carson Valley finally began to run out.

The Nevada economy fell apart, and thousands of people left, in search of work in other parts of the country, such as California. The state's population fell from 62,000 in 1880 to just 47,000 in 1890. Many communities were simply abandoned, to become the ghost towns that are now scattered across Nevada. Many Nevada ghost towns—such as Rhyolite and Goldfield, west of Las Vegas, and Chloride, near the Hoover Dam—are now tourist attractions.

Rhyolite, a gold mining town near Beatty, had a population of 10,000 in 1908. Just seven years later, in 1915, the gold had run out and only about twenty people were left.

The boom-and-bust cycle started all over again in 1900, when Jim Butler, a rancher in central Nevada, went looking for a stray burro. He discovered a rich vein of silver. Within two years, a town called Tonopah had grown up around the find. The town had about three thousand residents. The mines of the Tonopah eventually produced silver valued at $125 million. But

The once-busy mining center of Tonopah is now a ghost town.

when the silver ran out, so did Tonopah's days as "Queen of the Silver Camps." Today, only about fifty people live there.

Nevada's mines were producing incredible wealth, but most of the people who worked in them remained very poor. In 1907, miners in the town of Goldfield, near Tonopah, grew angry over low pay and dangerous working conditions. They went on strike and refused to work in the mines until their lives were improved. The Tonopah-Goldfield strike, the bitterest labor conflict in the state's history, ended only when President Theodore Roosevelt sent in the U.S. Army.

Modern Nevada

Nevada was hit hard by the Great Depression, an economic collapse that began in 1929 and caused widespread unemployment. The federal government tried to create jobs with "make work" projects. These projects gave people jobs building roads, cutting down trees in the forest, and doing other things that would help to improve the country. One of these projects

Huge dynamite blasts cleared away tons of rock to make room for the Hoover Dam.

began in 1931. It was a huge dam across the Colorado River. At first, this dam was called the Boulder Dam. It was later renamed the Hoover Dam after Herbert Hoover, who was president when the project was first approved.

The construction of the Hoover Dam took five years, five thousand workers, and more than seven million tons of concrete. An entire community, Boulder City, was built to house the workers and their families. The Hoover Dam project helped bring Nevada's economy back to life.

Another decision made in 1931 helped Nevada's economy. Lawmakers in the state decided to make gambling legal, for the first time since 1910. Gambling was against the law in most of the country, and Nevada's new casinos soon became a popular attraction for out-of-state visitors with money to spend.

Nowhere did the changes have a greater impact than in the sleepy desert town known as Las Vegas. The first casino in Las Vegas was built in 1931. But the city in those days was nothing like what it is today. Charles Miles, a resident of Las Vegas since 1932, remembers being a five-year-old in the city: "It was a little railroad town at that time—a place where everybody knew everybody and nobody ever locked their doors. It really was a great place to be a kid."

Few people saw Las Vegas's potential until 1946, when Benjamin "Bugsy" Siegel, a gangster from New York, opened

> The name Las Vegas is Spanish for "The Meadows."

the Flamingo, a flashy hotel and casino. The Flamingo eventually became a huge success, and in the years that followed, more casinos opened up in Las Vegas. The greatest stars of the entertainment world at that time—from Frank Sinatra to Elvis Presley—came to play on the stages of Las Vegas. These performances attracted even more people to the casinos and the gaming tables, bringing more money into Nevada.

The trouble was that much of the money was going into the wrong pockets. Many of the hotels and casinos of Las Vegas were owned or controlled by criminal organizations. These were large gangs, run almost like normal businesses. Many of them based in the big cities such as New York and Chicago. The federal government began investigating the gambling industry, and found that many of the establishments in Las Vegas were not paying their taxes or were being managed illegally.

The federal and state governments were determined to clean up the state's gambling industry. In 1967 a change in Nevada law allowed big corporations to invest in the state's casinos for the first time. That meant gambling became more of a normal business with fewer criminal elements.

In 1951, the United States government began to test nuclear bombs in Nevada. Nevada was chosen because it offered a huge land area where almost no one lived. Now known as the Nevada Test Site, this area covers about 1,375-square-miles of desert—an area bigger than the entire state of Rhode Island. The site is just 65 miles northwest of Las Vegas. Here, at a desolate spot called Frenchman's Flat, the United States government has conducted most of its nuclear weapons tests.

In the early days of nuclear testing, most Americans believed it was good for the country. The Soviet Union and

some other countries were developing nuclear weapons, and the United States wanted to be able to defend itself if there was a nuclear war. But many people were not aware of the long-term effects of radiation, which is given off by these weapons. Radiation can cause many serious health problems, including cancer.

Nevadans worry about the long-term impact, on the environment and on their

Between 1951 and 1993, 928 atomic bombs were exploded at the Nevada Test Site.

3 The People

For thousands of years, Nevada did not have an extremely large population. Even today, parts of the state have very few people. And yet, in the past few decades, Nevada's population has exploded. Year after year, millions of people come to Nevada. The explosive growth in Nevada's population makes clear that many people are drawn to this land, and to the spirit of these people.

In 1950, fewer than 160,000 people lived in the Silver State. Just ten years later, the Census Bureau reported that Nevada had a population of almost 285,000. That made the state the fastest-growing state in the country—a position it has held ever since. Today, Nevada's population is estimated to be about 2,240,000.

In the 1990s, Nevada's population increased by 66.3 percent, which is more than three times the national average. This means that Nevada the highest proportion of new arrivals—people who have come from somewhere else—of any state. Most of these new residents settle in Clark County, the area

A bronco rider tests his skill, and his courage, at a rodeo in Reno.

Las Vegas is the fastest-growing city in Nevada. More than 75,000 new residents arrived in Las Vegas in 2002 alone.

that includes Las Vegas. Almost three-quarters of a million people settled in the county in the ten years between 1990 and 2000.

They come from all over the world, and all over the country. But every year, about a third of them come from just one place: right next door, in California. Estéban Kolsky, a technology analyst who moved to Reno from Los Angeles in 1999, says, "We've seen many new people coming from California, especially since the end of the high-tech boom in 2001. There's plenty of work, you can buy a house for a fraction of what it would cost in San Francisco or L.A.—and the quality of life here is a big attraction, too."

Diversity

The new Nevadans have changed the Silver State in many ways, making it a more diverse place than it was in the past. Nonwhites have been here for thousands of years, of course. The first Nevadans, the Native Americans, experienced a long, tragic decline after the arrival of white people. They were often forced off the land their ancestors had lived on for centuries. They now make up one of the smallest—and poorest—minority groups in the state.

Native Americans now make up slightly more than 1 percent of Nevada's population. Many of them still live on reservations, such as the Duck Valley Reservation, which covers almost 300,000 acres on the Nevada-Idaho border and is home to more than 1,200 Paiute and Shoshone. In recent years Nevada's Native Americans have increased their political influence, fighting in the courts to take back land they believe was unfairly taken from them. In 1970, a federal court awarded the Southern Paiute millions of dollars to settle one of these court actions. The Native Americans of Nevada have used the money they have gained in this way to build new businesses that bring in money, taxes, and jobs. One of these businesses is the Las Vegas Paiute Resort, which has three of the finest golf courses in the world. Other groups own

The Native Americans of Nevada are working hard to preserve their special traditions. This Shoshone baby is carried in a traditional cradleboard.

cattle ranches and mining operations. Perhaps most important, they have worked hard to keep their traditional culture alive, with museums, festivals, and powwows, which are traditional Native American gatherings, with music, dancing, and storytelling.

African Americans, too, have been here since the first days of the "white" settlers—many of whom were not white at all. In 1850, James Pierson Beckwourth, a mountain man who had been born into slavery in Virginia, discovered an important path for wagon trains through the Sierra Nevada, to California. This path is known as the Beckwourth Trail. Benjamin Palmer, another former slave, is believed to have been the first African-American settler in Nevada. He built a 400 acre ranch near Sheridan in 1853, and worked it for more than forty years. Today African Americans now make up almost 7 percent of the Silver State's population.

The Hispanic, or Spanish-speaking, population of Nevada is exploding, too. Nevada's Hispanic population nearly doubled in the 1990s, and Nevada is now one of the ten "most Hispanic" states in the country. Almost 20 percent of the population is of Hispanic ancestry.

The Basques are a prominent ethnic group in Nevada. Most Nevadans who are Basque have ancestors who came to the state from Spain. Many Basques saw a resemblance between northern Nevada and their homes in the Pyrenees region, which is on the border between Spain and France. When they arrived, many settled in the northern part of the

In 1873, a Basque immigrant named Pedro Altube founded the Spanish Ranch, a huge cattle operation in the Independence Valley. He brought so many of his friends and relatives to America that he is known as the "Father of the Basques in the West."

state around Reno, Elko, and Winnemucca. Many took up their traditional occupations, becoming sheepherders and, eventually, successful sheep ranchers. Modern Basques in Nevada have also built many hotels. One of the great pleasures of a drive across Nevada today is stopping at a small-town hotel for a Basque meal. This meal could include traditional foods such as chorizo (spiced pork sausage), garbanzo beans, and grilled lamb.

The Basque culture is very old and distinct and the Basque language is believed to be unrelated to any other language in the world. Like other cultures, the state's Basques have their own traditions and festivals. They honor their heritage with celebrations that include dancing, food, and other traditional activities.

Children of Basque ancestry perform a traditional dance.

Recipe for Basque Garlic and Bread Soup

This traditional Basque recipe turns bread into a delicious, hearty soup. It is simple to make, but you will need an adult to help you cut the food and use the stove.

Ingredients:

1/2 cup olive oil

6 garlic cloves, sliced thin

1/2 slightly hardened
   baguette (French bread),
   cut into thin slices

4 cups water or chicken broth

6 large eggs

Paprika

Salt

Pepper

Have an adult help you heat the olive oil in a heavy pot or skillet over medium heat. Add the garlic and stir it for two to three minutes using a wooden spoon. The garlic should become a rich golden color—be careful not the burn the mixture. Add the bread, and turn it several times so that it absorbs the oil. Sprinkle in some paprika and mix it well.

Add the water or broth, and cook for 10 to 15 minutes. Continue to stir it until the soup is heated through. The bread should soak up a lot of the liquid. You can add some salt or pepper to the soup if you like.

Once the soup is heated, have an adult help you crack the eggs, and slide them onto the surface of the soup. You must be sure not to break the yolks. Cook the soup for at least another five minutes—you must make sure the eggs are fully cooked. The yolks should be firm, not runny, and you should not be able to see through the whites.

Serve the soup by spooning it gently into shallow bowls, allowing 1 egg per serving. Dig in and enjoy!

Many Asian immigrants have also come to Nevada. Some are Asian Americans who have moved from other states. Others are from Asian countries such as India, China, Japan, and the Philippines. Some Asian Nevadans are descendants of the Chinese who came to the region more than one hundreds years ago. Most of those early immigrants came to work on the railroads. In those days they faced terrible discrimination from white residents and other immigrants. As with many immigrants, it was very difficult for those early Chinese residents to own land and run their businesses. Today, however, Chinese Americans and other Asian Americans have thriving businesses. Many of Nevada's Asian communities have their own restaurants, food stores, and cultural festivals. Every January, Las Vegas celebrates the Asian New Year with a Chinese lion dance, Japanese taiko drums, and other Asian traditions.

Most of the people from different states or from different cultures came to Nevada to work, and work hard. But they also came for Nevada's special way of life. Many were drawn to the fast-paced life of Las Vegas. Others liked the slower pace of the state's small towns and suburban areas. And some wanted it all: exciting cities, just a few miles away from untouched wilderness areas. They all found what they were looking for in the Silver State.

But many of the people who come to live in Nevada today do not work at all, because they are retired. Nevada has one of the largest retired populations in the United States. Retirees from all over the country come to Nevada because of the many exciting recreational activities, the low cost of living, and, of course, the warm, sunny weather. Many live in special retirement communities, where they can be close to other people their own age.

Famous Nevadans

Sarah Winnemucca Hopkins:
Native American Activist and Writer

Sarah Winnemucca Hopkins was the daughter of a great Northern Paiute chief. She was born in 1844 and spent many years working to protect Native American rights. Early in her life, she worked as a translator for the U.S. Army. Later, she gave lectures and met with political leaders to raise awareness of the mistreatment of Native Americans. Her 1883 autobiography, Life among the Piutes: Their Wrongs and Claims, *is thought to be the first book ever published by a Native American woman. Sarah Winnemucca Hopkins died in 1891.*

Andre Agassi: Tennis Player

Andre Agassi was born in Las Vegas in 1970. He learned to play tennis from his father, an Armenian immigrant who worked as a waiter in Las Vegas hotels. Agassi trained hard and soon became one of the greatest players in the history of the game. He is one of only five players who have won all four of tennis's "grand slam" events—Wimbledon and the Australian, French, and U.S. Opens—he also won a gold medal at the 1996 Olympics in Atlanta.

Greg LeMond: Cyclist

The world of international bicycle racing had always been dominated by Europeans, until 1983, when a young man from Reno named Greg LeMond won the world championship. In 1986, LeMond went on to win one of cycling's greatest events, the three-week, 2,500-mile Tour de France. Despite being badly hurt in a hunting accident, LeMond came back to win the Tour twice more, and to become a world champion again.

Wovoka

Early in 1889, Wovoka—a young Paiute also known as Jack Wilson—believed that God had spoken to him and told him that Native Americans would no longer be troubled by white men if they performed a sacred dance. Wovoka's message was one of peace. He was hoping that Native Americans could once again live free on their land as they had before white settlement. Wovoka's teachings came to be known as the Ghost Dance Movement and spread among the Native Americans of the West. The Ghost Dance helped inspire a rebellion among the Lakota Native Americans. Unfortunately, the uprising ended in tragedy on December 29, 1890, when the U.S. Cavalry killed almost two hundred men, women, and children at Wounded Knee, in South Dakota.

Dolora Zajick: Opera Singer

Dolora Zajick was born in Reno. Some of her early performances were as a part of the chorus of the Nevada Opera. After studying music in New York, she went on to perform with the world's greatest opera companies, including the Metropolitan Opera in New York and La Scala in Milan, Italy. A mezzo-soprano, Zajick is well known for performing the rich dramatic roles of the Italian composer Giuseppe Verdi.

Anne Martin: Activist

Anne Martin was the first woman to make a serious attempt to be elected to the United States Senate. Born in Empire in 1875, she became a teacher at Nevada State University. Martin became interested in the suffrage movement, which wanted women to get the right to vote. Partly as a result of her efforts, Nevada's women received the right to vote in 1914. Martin ran for the Senate twice, in 1918 and 1920, but did not win.

The many changes in Nevada in recent years have made it a fascinating and complicated place. The modern world is very closely linked to the natural environment here. Even the glittering hotels and casinos of Las Vegas and Reno are just a few minutes away from the natural beauty of the desert and the mountains.

Many Nevadans, in fact, barely even notice the neon-lit attractions the tourists love. Some prefer hiking in the desert, visiting a museum, or enjoying local attractions, such as local festivals.

In many ways, the people of Nevada have the best of all worlds. They treasure their pioneer heritage, and the untouched beauty of the wilderness. At the same time, they are very proud of the rapid pace of progress in the Silver State—and of all the opportunities it brings them. Like people everywhere, they worry about some of the effects of progress. But most Nevadans share great confidence in their state, and believe that its future will be just as rich and exciting as its past.

In Nevada, even the sky is full of fun things to do and see.

A rancher herds his cattle. Many Nevadans still live close to the land, just as the first settlers did.

The People

Calendar of Events

National Cowboy Poetry Gathering

Every January, the town of Elko, in the heart of cowboy country, celebrates its old West heritage. That means big hats, big boots, big stories (some folks might even call them tall tales), and, of course, poetry.

Jim Butler Days

Once a year—usually on the Memorial Day weekend, at the end of May—Tonopah remembers the man who went looking for a lost burro, and started the last great Nevada mining rush. Activities include a big parade and a street dance.

National Cowboy Poetry Gathering

National Basque Festival

The Basques of Nevada say, "Ongi etorri" or "Welcome," with this grand celebration of their traditional culture, every July in Elko. The high point is the "running from the bulls," when lots of people let themselves be chased through the streets by real live bulls.

Nevada Indian Days All Indian Rodeo & Pow Wow

Native Americans from all over the state gather in Fallon in July, for rodeo events and traditional singing, dancing, games, crafts, and food and drink.

Nevada State Fair

The Nevada State Fair is held in Reno in August. It is nearly as old as the state itself. Every year since 1874, people from all over the state have gathered for food, fun, and a celebration of Nevada's rich heritage.

Spirit of Wovoka Days

Every August, the town of Yerington, on the Walker River, celebrates the legacy of Wovoka, the great Paiute mystic and founder of the Ghost Dance movement. Among the highlights of this pow wow are traditional shawl and bustle dances by members of many different Native American groups.

Virginia City Camel Races

This annual event, in Virginia City in September, looks back at a time when camels were used to carry freight to and from the mines of the Comstock Lode

National Championship Air Races and Air Show

A pow wow in Reno

Every September, the skies above Reno roar with the sounds of different kinds of aircraft, from World War II fighters to racing jets.

Nevada Day Celebration

Carson City celebrates the day Nevada became a state—October 31, 1864—with a parade and lots of other festivities. Many of the events, like the World Championship Rock Drilling Contest, recall the Silver State's mining past.

National Finals Rodeo

For one week in December, Las Vegas becomes "the cowboy capital of the world." This annual event—with bareback riding, calf roping, and much, much more—is the most important event on the rodeo circuit.

4 How It Works

The people of Nevada are represented by three different levels of government: local, state, and federal. Each of these levels is, in its own way, extremely important.

The state's cities, towns, and villages all have their own local governments. Most have mayors and city or town councils, which are elected by local voters every two years. They make decisions about property taxes, schools, and other local issues. Nevada is also divided into seventeen counties, managed by boards of commissioners that are elected every two years. An example of one of a county government's responsibilities is maintaining police departments.

Nevada's Native American reservations have their own distinct forms of government. The residents choose their leaders, who are responsible for police and fire services, road repairs, and other important services.

Nevada's state government, which makes decisions that affect the entire state, is based on a system of "checks and

The Capitol, in Carson City, is the home of Nevada's state government.

balances." This means that the three separate parts of the state government—executive, legislative, and judicial—watch over each other, to make sure that laws are passed smoothly and that none of the branches has more power than the other.

Branches of Government

Executive The executive branch, headed by the governor, handles the day-to-day management of the state and makes sure that Nevada's laws and regulations are properly enforced. The governor and the other senior officials of the executive branch—governor, secretary of state, treasurer, and controller—are elected by all the voters in the state. These officials serve four-year terms, and cannot hold office for more than two terms.

Legislative The legislative branch creates new state laws, and makes changes to existing laws. Nevada's legislative branch has two houses: the forty-two-member assembly and the twenty-one-member senate. Members of the assembly serve two-year terms, while members of the senate serve for four years. Both are elected by the voters of their individual state electoral districts.

Judicial The judicial branch—the court system—makes sure that Nevada's laws are properly interpreted and enforced. The highest level of the judicial branch, the state supreme court, hears appeals from the lower courts, and decides whether new laws agree with Nevada's constitution. The supreme court has a chief justice and six associate justices, who are elected for six-year terms. Thirty-five district court justices, who are also elected for six years, hear important criminal and civil cases. There are also municipal and small claims courts that handle less serious cases.

Making Laws

The members of the Nevada state assembly and senate are often asked to pass new laws, or change existing ones. When someone in the legislature decides that he or she wants to do this, he or she proposes a new law—called a bill—and a legislative attorney prepares a draft version of the bill.

Then a committee from one of the houses considers the draft bill, and decides to send it to the appropriate house. (If a committee belongs to the senate, then they send the bill to the senate. If a committee belongs to the assembly, the bill is presented to the assembly.) Most of these committees have a special focus, such as education, taxes, or agriculture. The members of the committee discuss the details of the bill. They usually make changes, called amendments. If they believe the bill is a good thing, they present it to one of the houses, which debates it and then votes on it.

The assembly and senate meet in the Legislative Building.

If the house approves, or passes, the draft bill, it goes to the other house, where the whole process begins again. Sometimes, if there are differences of opinion between the two houses, the bill may be sent to a joint conference committee. This committee, which includes representatives from both houses, tries to create a compromise version of the bill. This new bill is then presented to both houses for a vote.

To become law, a bill must be approved in a vote by a majority of the members of both houses. This requires eleven votes in the assembly, and twenty-two in the senate. Once the bill has been approved, it is sent to the governor, who either signs it, making it a law, or vetoes—rejects—it. The legislature can override the governor's veto, by giving it a two-thirds majority in another vote.

Nevadans can also create laws directly, using the initiative process. If enough people sign a petition, an initiative is placed on the ballot during statewide elections. A majority of voters must approve a petition, and they must do it twice, in two election years.

The Federal Government in Nevada

Nevada is also represented in the federal government, in Washington, D.C. The state's voters elect two senators, and three members of the House of Representatives. (Nevada gained one more representative in 2000, because of its growing population.) Representation at the federal level is especially important in Nevada, because the federal government is unusually powerful here.

The U.S. government owns or controls more than 85 percent of the land in Nevada, in the form of military bases, national parks, and other holdings. There is often conflict between Nevadans and the federal government. A rancher who wants to herd cattle on a particular piece of land may have to deal with many different federal agencies, for example, the Bureau of Land Management, the Fish and Wildlife Service, the Forest Service, even the military.

One government activity probably bothers Nevadans more than any other: The use of the desert as a place to test nuclear weapons and store the leftover waste materials from them. Nevadans' nuclear concerns became even more serious in 1987, when the federal government announced plans to create a huge $58 billion storage area for nuclear waste at Yucca Mountain, at the edge of the Nevada Test Site. The plan called for seventy-seven thousand tons of radioactive material—such as spent fuel from nuclear power plants—to be stored at Yucca Mountain.

Despite years of government assurances that Yucca Mountain would be safe, the majority of Nevadans—more than 70 percent, according to some opinion polls—opposed the plan. Nonetheless, on July 23, 2002, President George W. Bush signed a law approving the Yucca Mountain plan.

"Nevada considers the Yucca Mountain project to be the product of extremely bad science, extremely bad law, and extremely bad public policy."
—Nevada governor Kenny Guinn

Many Nevadans opposed the Yucca Mountain nuclear storage plan.

How You Can Make a Difference

Nevadan's failure to stop Yucca Mountains shows that nobody can win every battle. Still, if there is an issue you care about, you should get involved. The best way to start is by learning as much as you can about the issue. You can do this by reading your local newspaper, following the news on television, the radio, or the Internet, and talking to parents and teachers.

Your next step should be to contact your representatives in the local, state, or federal government—or all three—to make sure your voice is heard. You can do this by letter, by E-mail, by telephone, or even in person.

When the state legislature is in session, you can watch debates and sit in on committee meetings. (Nevada state legislators officially convene or meet every two years. You can also make an appointment to visit your representatives at their offices. Nevada's population is still small enough that people sometimes just go to the silver-domed capitol in Carson City and tell their lawmakers what is on their minds. It is just another way the Silver State keeps in touch with its pioneer roots.

To find Nevada's state senators'
contact information go to:
http://www.leg.state.nv.us/72nd/legislators/senators/slist.cfm.
To find your state assembly member:
http://www.leg.state.nv.us/72nd/legislators/assembly/alist.cfm.
You will need to know which district you live in. Ask a teacher,
librarian, or parent to help you find your district.

5 Making a Living

The people of Nevada make their living in many different ways, both old and new. A typical Nevada worker might be a hotel desk clerk in Lake Tahoe, a cowboy on a ranch outside Elko, a teacher, a shop owner, or a construction worker building a new housing project in Las Vegas. Nevada's expanding economy needs all these types of workers—and many more.

From the Land

Despite the stunning changes the past few decades have brought, Nevada has not left behind all its traditional ways of making a living. Mining is still a very important industry here. Open-pit and underground mines use highly advanced technologies to find precious metals such as gold and silver, semiprecious stones such as turquoise and opals, and construction materials including gypsum, limestone, and clays.

Today's mining is not the same backbreaking work it was in the 1800s. Today, satellite images may be used to locate mineral deposits. Remote-control digging equipment means that miners

Tourism is the backbone of the Nevada economy.

Huge mines—such as this gold mine—use advanced technology to extract mineral wealth from the earth.

do not have to go into dangerous underground areas. But this modern technology means that Nevada's mines do not need as many workers as they used to. Only about 5 percent of Nevada workers are now employed in the mining industry.

More than 50 million ounces of gold have been extracted from the Carlin Trend, a forty-mile line that cuts across northeastern Nevada. Geologists believe that at least 107 million ounces still lies beneath the earth there.

Agriculture has always been tough in Nevada, and it now represents only about 1 percent of the state's economy. But there are some 1,700 cattle and sheep ranches scattered across the Silver State, and about three thousand farms. The meat and wool they produce are shipped all over the world.

Hardworking men and women watch over the herd at this cattle ranch.

Nevada's farms grow food crops, such as potatoes and onions, and livestock feed like barley and hay. In places where irrigation and conservation projects ensure an abundant supply of water, farmers can even grow crops that would not ordinarily grow in a climate as dry as Nevada's, like tomatoes and grapes. Many of the state's agricultural products are sold locally, but farm and ranch products are also exported to other states and other countries. Agriculture is still a small part of the state's economy, but it is still worth more than $350 million every year.

The Newlands Project—the first irrigation project ever built by the U.S. government—diverted the waters of the Carson and Truckee rivers. The 1903 to 1908 project brought water, and farming, to an 87,000-acre stretch of desert through a long series of canals, dams, and irrigation ditches.

A machinist at work in a factory near Las Vegas

Other industries continue to grow in Nevada. Manufacturing is becoming a more important segment of the state's economy, especially in Reno, Henderson, and North Las Vegas. The state's central position in the West, and its excellent, ultramodern transportation system, make the state—especially the area around the old railroad town of Sparks—a center for warehousing. Many large companies store goods here while waiting to ship them to their customers all over the country. These goods may include cars and trucks from Detroit, electronics from Japan, or computer software from California. When the time is right, they will be shipped to waiting customers in all fifty states.

Nevada

Plenty of new businesses open up in Nevada every year, and lots of others move here from other states, attracted by skilled workers, low costs, and—probably most important of all—low taxes. Nevadans pay less tax than the residents of almost any other state. There are no state taxes on what people earn from their jobs, on the profits their businesses make, or on money they inherit from their families.

These factory workers are making electronic gambling machines to be used in Nevada casinos.

Products & Resources

Gold

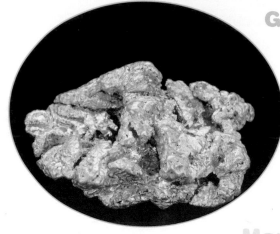

Nevada's early economy was built on silver mining, but today, gold is an even more important resource. The state is the third-richest source of gold in the world, after South Africa.

Manufacturing

Nevada's fast-growing manufacturing sector is concentrated mostly around Reno and the Las Vegas suburbs of Henderson and North Las Vegas. Nevada's manufacturers produce computer software, aircraft parts, plastics and chemicals, printing products, and—not surprisingly—gambling equipment.

Tourism

The tourism industry is by far Nevada's most important. Outdoor activities are populat attractions. The cities are, too—Las Vegas alone welcomed more than 35 million visitors in 2002. These visitors spent more than $31 billion at the city's hotels, casinos, and other attractions.

Turquoise

Nevada produces more of this beautiful blue-green gemstone than any other state. Turquoise was a valuable trade item for the Native Americans of the Southwest, who now use it in handmade jewelry that is prized by collectors all over the world.

Transportation

A superb transportation system—road, land, and air—keeps people and goods moving in and out of Nevada. Las Vegas's McCarran International Airport handles 36 million passengers every year, which makes it the seventh-busiest in the world.

Water

No natural resource is more important to Nevada than water. Even though it is the driest state in the country, Nevada actually sends water to other places. The Hoover Dam irrigates more than a million acres of farmland, as far away as Mexico. Huge turbines at the Hoover Dam also turn the power of rushing water into electricity.

Teachers and childcare workers are part of Nevada's important service sector.

Service

More than 50 percent of Nevada's workers are employed in the service sector. Anyone who does something for someone else—instead of making a product—is a service worker. Doctors and lawyers, teachers and real estate agents, television repairmen and waiters, are all in service jobs. And one of the most important parts of Nevada's service industry is tourism

Tourism is the backbone of Nevada's economy. This industry brings in more than half of the state's income, just as it has for more than half a century. While many parts of Nevada are ideal for tourists, Las Vegas tends to pull in the most. More than 35 million people visit Las Vegas every year. The city has the ten largest hotels in the United States, and more hotel rooms than anywhere else in the world. Many of the hotels and resorts in Las Vegas are planned around certain themes. Some are designed to resemble cities in different countries One may be an exact replica of an ancient Egyptian pyramid, while another could look like nineteenth-century Paris or a tropical island. Most of the hotels in Las Vegas have casinos and other gambling opportunities. People who come to gamble in Las Vegas often spend an average of about $500 per visit at the gambling tables.

But people do not just visit Nevada to gamble. Over the past few years the state has become a great place for family vacations. There are many shows, concerts, and other forms of entertainment for the whole family to enjoy. Nevada has many resorts, spas, and golf courses that offer a fun and relaxing time.

Nevada—Las Vegas especially—has also become an ideal spot for business from other states and even other countries. With the large choices in hotels and resorts, many companies choose to have conferences and conventions in the state. "Las Vegas is a great place to do business," says Marjorie Buckmaster, a writer who often attends conferences in the city. "I mean, where else can you go to meetings in the morning, watch a pirate battle in the afternoon, then have dinner in the Eiffel Tower in the evening?"

Tourism in Nevada is not just about Las Vegas and Reno. More and more visitors come to visit Virginia City and other places that preserve memories of the old days of pioneers and silver miners. For these people, strolling through a ghost town like Rhyolite is much more fun than catching the floor show at a casino.

Other tourists are drawn by the natural beauty of wild Nevada. They come to backpack in the Sierra Nevada, water-ski on Lake Mead, or stare in wonder at an ancient bristlecone pine in Great Basin National Park.

All these visitors spend money in Nevada. And that creates jobs for everyone from tour guides to ski instructors, from bus drivers to airport baggage handlers.

Some parts of the state are entirely dependent upon tourism. In some parts of the Sierra Nevada, for example, the heavy winter snows mean that hotels, ski lodges, restaurants and the like are almost the only businesses that can really operate for several months of the year.

The tourism industry is almost constantly in need of workers. The people who come to Nevada to take these jobs also create new economic opportunity, because they need goods and services, everything from houses and microwave ovens to education and medical care. That, in turn, creates more jobs for others. The result is that Nevada's economy is now much more stable than it was in the days of the boom-and-bust cycle.

Nevada's workers are probably the state's most important resource. Their determination, drive, and energy show the same spirit as in Nevada's early days. The modern Nevadan is more likely to be employed by a resort hotel or a software company than a silver mine or a cattle ranch. But the old pioneer spirit still shows in their hard work and their welcoming smiles. The people of Nevada are the main reason so many visitors come to the Silver State—and will keep coming for many years.

Hikers enjoy the natural beauty of Mount Charleston, just a short distance from Las Vegas.

The Nevada state flag has a cobalt-blue background. In the upper left-hand corner is a five-pointed silver star with the word Nevada in gold below it. Above the star is a gold scroll with the words BATTLE BORN. To the right and left of the star are sprays of sagebrush.

Nevada's official seal shows the words The Great Seal of the State of Nevada in a circle on a cobalt-blue field. Inside the circle is a picture of farm equipment, a mine, and a steam train, with the sun rising above mountains in the background. A scroll beneath the picture bears Nevada's state motto: "All for Our Country."

NEVADA

New Year Lake

Sheldon National Wildlife Refuge

Fort McDermitt Indian Reservation

Duck Valley Indian Reservation

Owyhee

Humboldt-Toiyabe National Forest

BILK CREEK

140

Summit Lake Indian Reservation

KINGS RIVER MOUNTAINS

SANTA ROSA RANGE

OWYHEE DESERT

Humboldt-Toiyabe National Forest

225

DESERT VALLEY

95

INDEPENDENCE MOUNTAINS

Wells

80

BLACK ROCK DESERT

Quinn River

Humboldt River

Humboldt River

Winnemucca

Elko

Spring Creek

Snow Water Lake

West Wendover

Pyramid Lake Indian Reservation

THE LAVA BEDS

Rye Patch Reservoir

Battle Mountain

SHOSHONE RANGE

Huntington River

Humboldt-Toiyabe National Forest

93

Goshute Indian Reservation

80

TRINITY RANGE

Humboldt River

Lovelock

STILLWATER RANGE

Humboldt Salt Marsh

CLAN ALPINE MOUNTAINS

278

RUBY MOUNTAINS

South Fork Indian Reservation

Humboldt-Toiyabe National Forest

Sparks

95

305

TOIYABE RANGE

Hickison Petroglyph Recreation Area

Duck River

Reno

Fallon

Fallon Indian Reservaton

Eureka

50

Ely

SNAKE RANGE

Great Basin National Park

Silver Springs

Carson City

Walker River Indian Reservation

MONITOR RANGE

Humboldt-Toiyabe National Forest

RUTH COPPER PIT

Humboldt-Toiyabe National Forest

Lake Tahoe

Stateline

Lahontan Reservoir

Berlin Ichthyosaur State Park

Duckwater Indian reservation

6

Topaz Lake

Walker Lake

Humboldt-Toiyabe National Forest

LUNAR CRATER

Humboldt-Toiyabe National Forest

White River

93

Humboldt-Toiyabe National Forest

Hawthorne

95

376

375

LEVIATHAN CAVE GEOLOGICAL AREA

Cathedral Gorge State Park

Caliente

EXCELSIOR MOUNTAINS

BOUNDARY PEAK

NATIONAL WILDHORSE MANAGEMENT AREA

Pahranagat National Wildlife Refuge

DELAMAR MOUNTAINS

MEADOW VALLEY WASH

Tonopah

NEVADA MILITARY TEST SITE

DESERT NATIONAL WILDLIFE RANGE

Mesquite

Death Valley National Park

Beatty

95

AMARGOSA DESERT

Humboldt-Toiyabe National Forest

SHEEP RANGE

Moapa Indian Reservation

Overton

Lake Mead National Recreation Area

Mt. Charleston Wilderness Area

15

GYPSUM CAVE

Lake Mead

Pahrump

Las Vegas

Henderson

Hoover Dam

Sandy Valley

Colorado River

95

Lake Mohave

Laughlin

miles
0   30

N
W   E
S

Legend

Interstate Highway	State Capital	Highest Point in the State	National Forest	Indian Reservation
U.S. Highway	City or Town	Mountains	National Park	Recreation Area
State Highway	Wildlife Refuge	State Park	Wilderness Area	

Home Means Nevada

Words and Music by
Bertha Raffetto

'Way out in the land of the set - ting sun, Where the wind blows wild and free, There's a

love - ly spot, just the on - ly one That means home sweet home to me. If you

fol - low the old Kit Car - son trail, Un - til des - ert meets the hills, Oh you

cer - tain - ly will a - gree with me, It's the place of a thou - sand thrills.

CHORUS

Home, means Ne - va - da, Home, means the hills, Home, means the sage and the pines.

Out by the Truck - ee's sil - ver - y rills, Out where the sun al - ways shines,

There is the land that I love the best, Fair - er than all I can see.

Right in the heart of the gold - en west Home, means Ne - va - da to me.

State Song

More About Nevada

Books

Stefoff, Rebecca. *Celebrate the States: Nevada*. New York: Benchmark Books, 2001.

Stein, R. Conrad. *Nevada*. New York: Children's Press, 2000.

Lillegard, Dee and Wayne Stoker. *Nevada*. New York: Children's Press, 1991.

Web sites

Complete Nevada Traveler

http://www.nevadaweb.com/cnt/index.html

Nevada History—A Walk in the Past

http://www.nevada-history.org/

Nevada State Library and Archives—Historical Myth a Month

http://dmla.clan.lib.nv.us/docs/nsla/archives/myth/

About the Author

Terry Allan Hicks has written books for Marshall Cavendish on subjects ranging from the Declaration of Independence to the state of New Hampshire. He lives in Connecticut with his wife, Nancy, and their sons, Jamie, Jack, and Andrew.

Index

Page numbers in **boldface** are illustrations.